HYPERTENSION
AND HEMODIALYSIS:
The Silent Treatment on the Rise!

Lakiesha Simpson - EL CCHT

authorHOUSE®

AuthorHouse™
1663 Liberty Drive
Bloomington, IN 47403
www.authorhouse.com
Phone: 833-262-8899

Published by AuthorHouse 01/07/2022

ISBN: 978-1-6655-4483-2 (sc)
ISBN: 978-1-6655-4482-5 (e)

Library of Congress Control Number: 2021923500

Print information available on the last page.

Any people depicted in stock imagery provided by Getty Images are models, and such images are being used for illustrative purposes only. Certain stock imagery © Getty Images.

Scripture quotations marked KJV are from the Holy Bible, King James Version (Authorized Version). First published in 1611. Quoted from the KJV Classic Reference Bible, Copyright © 1983 by The Zondervan Corporation.

This book is printed on acid-free paper.

Because of the dynamic nature of the Internet, any web addresses or links contained in this book may have changed since publication and may no longer be valid. The views expressed in this work are solely those of the author and do not necessarily reflect the views of the publisher, and the publisher hereby disclaims any responsibility for them.

First and Foremost, giving all perfect praise to Father God Allah with my Moorish American Prayer:

> Allah, the Father of the Universe, the Father of Love, Truth, Peace, Freedom and Justice, Allah is my Protector, my Guide, and my Salvation by night and by day through his Holy Prophet Drew Ali. Amen
> —*The Holy Koran of the Moorish Science Temple of America,* Circle 7, divinely prepared by the Noble Prophet Drew Ali

CONTENTS

FOREWORD

This book was thought out with divine love and kindness for our people, our communities, and our children for generations to come. It is meant to spread the light on a curable, treatable, and preventable disease that can be eradicated through proper nutrition, mental, physical, emotional, spiritual, and overall well-being as a whole person.

I wanted to share my expertise with being a Hemodialysis Technician along with my own personal experience with hypertension and how dialysis and hypertension relate to one another. Hypertension has damaging effects on specifically Asiatic (people identifying as black or African American) bodies, especially through traditional diets and lifestyles.

Dialysis and hypertension affect other cultures as well, but they specifically challenge Asiatic communities even more. I wanted to become a voice for this condition because the need is greater than ever. Dialysis centers are increasing around the country, and people between their twenties and fifties are being diagnosed with kidney disease at an alarming rate!

People are starting to get better control of their health and what they are putting in their bodies. There are more health stores with vegan and vegetarian meal options in grocery stores and restaurants. Health is improving, especially among younger generations. Dialysis is avoidable in most cases, and hypertension is preventable. With better dietary guidelines and food choices, there would be significant improvements in overall health.

The fallen sons and daughters of the Asiatic nation of North America need to learn to love instead of hate and get to know of their Higher selves and Lower selves. This is the uniting of the Holy Koran of Mecca for teaching and instructing all Moorish Americans.

The key to civilization is in the hands of the Asiatic nations:

- The Moors, who were the ancient Moabites, and founders of the Holy City of Mecca.
- The Egyptians, who were the Hamites, and of a direct descendant of Mizraim, the Arabians, the seed of Hager, Japanese, and Chinese.
- The Hindus of India, the descendants of the ancient Canaanites, Hittites, and Moabites from the land of Canaan.
- The Asiatic nations and countries in North, South, and Central America; the Moorish Americans and Mexicans in North America, and the Brazilians, Argentinians, and Chileans in South America.
- The Colombians, Nicaraguans, and natives of San Salvador in Central America. All of these are Moslems.
- The Turks are the true descendants of Hager, are the chief protectors of the Islamic Creed of Mecca, beginning with Mohammed the First, the founder of the uniting of Islam, by the command of the great universal God-Allah. (*Holy Koran*, Circle 7, chapter 47)

CHAPTER 1

The Eye of the Storm

I was born Lakiesha Lashawn Jones on July 14, 1986. I was raised on the East side of Detroit, Michigan. I was the only child raised by a wonderful, hardworking, tenacious single mother by the name of Cathy Ann Jones. My mother was a Laboratory Technician for more than twenty years. She was very skilled at the work she so passionately loved.

I had a very good childhood. We lived in a house on Courville Street with my grandmother, Annie, a registered nurse, and my two uncles and an auntie. My favorite uncle, Jerome, lived with us, He was a father figure to me, and I was his eldest niece. I was more like his daughter before he had children. I didn't feel neglected because my mother had help with raising me with alot of love and stability.

Our house was very big. It reminded me of a mini mansion so spacious and comfortable. I had everything I ever wanted as a child, from toys to plenty of cousins to play with on the weekends. Even the pagan holidays, like Easter, Thanksgiving, and Christmas, were celebrated in tip-top fashion every year.

When I was a young girl in grade school, my mother worked the midnight shift so that she could be home during the daytime to take me and pick me up from school. My mother also attended field trips and any other school activities that I was involved in. My mother displayed love and dedication for her only daughter which was greatly appreciated! My mother was also very strict. I wasn't allowed to do a lot of the things other children were doing, including going to friends' houses for sleepovers or being fast with boys. I can respect her for that because she was trying to protect her only child, and being conscious of making informed decisions made me a better young woman.

My grandmother was very strict too, but she was classy and sassy. She always wore her hair curled. I was my grandmother's eldest grandchild, and we were very close. She was more of a second mother to me, and I affectionately called her Ma or Mama. I used to always look forward to our trips down to South Carolina to visit long-distance family. I really loved her cooking, especially her Sunday dinners. Just like other Asiatic families, pork was a staple in our home: pork neck bones in a pot of greens, ham hocks in a pot of black-eyed peas and hot water cornbread, fried chicken and pinto or navy beans seasoned to perfection. Pepsi pop would wash it all down.

My grandmother encountered health issues, and she used to say that she had a "bad heart." She was a heavy smoker, and her favorite cigarettes were Virginia Slim Menthols. This was my first encountered with learning about sickness and disease. My grandmother suffered from angina, which is a symptom of coronary artery disease, which reduces blood flow in the heart's arteries. When I was six years old, she used to show me a small nitroglycerin pill to give her. It would restart her heart and open the arteries for blood flow and oxygen to her heart if it stopped. She told me to never play with this medicine and explained how dangerous it was if I took it.

October 2, 1993, would be the last day this six-year-old girl would affectionately call my grandmother "Ma." I was watching Saturday-morning cartoons on the downstairs couch with my uncle. He was asleep on one end of the couch, and I was on the opposite end. We heard a loud thump, and my uncle jumped up. We both ran upstairs. My uncle opened the door, and my grandmother's lifeless body was on the floor. Her eyes were fixed on the ceiling, and my aunt was performing CPR. My uncle moved me out of the way, and my mother, my aunt, and another uncle called 911. I frantically ran to my bedroom. I was crying and did not understand what was going on.

My cousin spent the night, and we went on to playing as we were instructed by the adults. The EMS arrived and took my grandmother's body to the ambulance on a gurney. Who would have known that was the last time I would see her.

My grandmother passed away from a massive heart attack at the age of fifty-two. That was very young. My grandmother had so much life ahead of her. She became an RN in her forties. She beat the odds of becoming a nurse, but heavy smoking and a poor diet took that all away.

I miss my grandmother very much, especially all the time we spent together I wanted to become a nurse just like her. She was the matriarch of my family, and it seemed like when she passed, the generational curse of poor diet and lifestyle was passed down. I learned a lot in my early years about how poor dietary choices and lifestyles lead to sickness and death, but I was too young to truly grasp how and why it happened.

The medical profession was prominent in my family, and as a young woman, I knew I wanted to become a medical professional like my grandmother and mother. In my adult years, I would find out what it was like to become a medical professional and see how poor diet and lifestyle and generational curses could affect my life.

I attended Jared Finney High School, where I was academic scholar and athlete. I ran track and field from my sophomore through senior year. Even though I was active, I developed high cholesterol because of bad eating habits.

Since I was an athlete, I thought I could just burn my favorite fattening foods and junk food and not gain weight or have health issues. I didn't take it seriously because I thought that the only way to get nutrition was from meat, potatoes, and carbs. I was focused on academics and sports and had normal teenager issues.

In the fall of 2004, I started my college career at Wayne State University. I contemplated becoming a medical professional as a science major. I have loved science since I was a little girl. I participated in the botany club, science fairs, and science projects. I was a science nerd, but I was proud of it. As a science major, I wanted to become a nurse or a biomedical engineer. Eventually my career choices changed, but I knew it would take a lot of patience and studying. I was devoted to science, and it took a lot of my time.

During my first year at Wayne State University, I gained a new interest. I met and fell in love with a wonderful young man named

Michael. Michael became my boyfriend, and our relationship was like a whirlwind romance. Michael was charming, smart, and respectful, and we continued to date. In 2009, I left Wayne State and transferred all my credits to Wayne County Community College.

While I was attending Wayne County Community College, my mother became gravely ill. She had congestive heart failure and kidney failure, and she started on dialysis in January 2010. I continued taking classes, and after school, I would visit my mother at the hospital. I also had a full-time job at Five Guys Burgers and Fries. I had to be in three places every day, and I was trying to better myself and look after my mother.

My mother's illness took a turn for the worse. Seven months later at the tender age of 46, on July 19, 2010 five days after my birthday my mother passed away. The pain and hurt was unforgettable! My mother was like a best friend to me, she taught me many life skills and lessons that I still hold dear in my heart to this day. My mother didn't have to suffer any longer, and I was at peace with planning and speaking at her funeral with my family because Allah gave me the strength to do so.

In November 2010, I got my first apartment in Clinton Township, Michigan and my first car, was a Chevy Malibu. As hard as it was, I knew I had to gain my independence and become a responsible adult. Michael was a loving and supportive boyfriend, and he was by my side every step of the way.

By 2011, Michael and I were ready to take the next step together. Michael asked my uncle Jerome for permission to marry me since he was the closest man to a father in my life. On June 18, 2011, Michael proposed to me, and we were happily engaged. In June 2012, I received my Associate of Science degree from Wayne County Community College, and I married Michael the love of my life on August 18th 2012.

That same year, sickness struck my family again. My uncle Jerome was ill with Leukemia. He started chemotherapy and was in and out of the hospital, but he was able to walk his eldest niece down the aisle. I was so honored because, despite his illness and weakness, he made the ultimate sacrifice any daddy would have done for their daughter.

My uncle passed away a year later on August 18, 2013 on Michael and I first wedding anniversary. I couldn't believe it. That day will always be a reminder that my uncle Jerome will always be with us. Our marriage and union together will always be something he was proud of.

The same year my uncle died, I found out I was pregnant. During my uncle's funeral, I was sporting a little baby bump. In my sadness and grief, though my uncle had transitioned, the thought of a new baby was coming was a blessing in disguise.

In October 2013, two months after my uncle's passing, during an ultrasound exam, Michael and I were told our baby's heart had stopped. The OB/GYN said that our baby wasn't vital and that I will have a miscarriage. The devastation and heartbreak tore us apart. How could this happen to us? I miscarried the baby at the apartment we were staying in at the time. Trying to stay positive, we held each other close and said we would try again. Two griefs in one year, I couldn't even imagine how much strength I really had. I was numb.

We moved out of our apartment and moved in with Michael's parents at the end of 2013 because we wanted to buy a home of our own. They welcomed me in as a daughter with loving and open arms.

In September 2014, I was pregnant again. This time, the pregnancy was vital. Our baby was growing strong inside of me. My mother-in-law cooked hearty meals for us, I was really fortunate to have her in my life, although I wished it was my own mother who was cooking and looking after her daughter and unborn grandson. I'm thankful to Allah for my mother-in-law and my father-in-law. On May 16, 2015, I gave birth to a healthy baby boy. Our first son Michael III is affectionately known as MJ. We moved into our new home in June 2015 as a family of three.

I started working again. I was trying to get my foot in the door in the medical field. I started as a dietary aide at Cherrywood Nursing Home in February 2016. I would spend time with seniors and serve them hot and cold beverages and food and snacks during mealtimes. It was my first time working with helping patients or feeding them nutritious food. I really enjoyed serving the elders and talking with them about their lives and families before they moved to the nursing home. I stayed there until September 2016.

I started seeking another position in the medical field. I applied on websites and at medical clinics. I wanted a career that I could really enjoy. In November 2016, I started working as a plane cabin cleaner at the Detroit Metropolitan Airport. My job duties were cleaning large aircraft, such as the Boeing 747, smaller jet engines, and the Airbus 380. It was amazing to clean the jumbo jets with other team members in between flights, and it was even more amazing to see them land at the airport or take off into the sunset. However, cleaning the planes was physically demanding. I had to pop the seats to clean in between them, check for weapons and bombs, and clean up mounds of trash from passengers flying from across the world on twelve- and eighteen-hour flights. I even found international coins and reading materials.

It was time-consuming, but it was a stepping-stone to getting to where I wanted to be in my career. I only stayed at the airport until March 2017, but I still had a longing for the medical field. In April 2017, I started working as a medical receptionist at St. John Hospital. I filed patient medical records, scheduled patient appointment times, and checked patients in and out before and after their appointments. I only stayed there until May because I got a phone call for dialysis technician training with Greenfield Health System. I was so elated with tears of joy and sadness because I had never thought about being a dialysis technician, especially with my mother being on dialysis, but there I was.

I began my eight-week course to train as a Hemodialysis Technician, and I was finally on my career path in the medical field. During my training, I was nervous but determined. My on-the-floor training began at Northwest Dialysis Unit. I began slowly, but I began to get comfortable with the patients, which made them feel at ease. I provided the best treatment possible to them.

In May 2017, I was placed at West Pavilion Outpatient Dialysis unit, which is one of the biggest dialysis units in Detroit. We see three hundred patients a week and sometimes more, and the workload definitely took some time to get used to. My first year at West Pavilion, I struggled to adapt to my job duties. I wanted to quit every day. As a new tech, I had to learn my way around the unit. I had a preceptor who was patient with me and taught me well. I began to follow my own lead and became familiar with patients and their accesses. I learned safe fluid removal, taking my time, and being more efficient with my workload.

I was learning as much as I could on the floor. I was asking nurses and technicians questions and what to do in most situations with patients. In 2017, I was pregnant with my second son, Deshawn, who is affectionately known as Das. I worked on the busy floor and was as careful as I could. I didn't want to quit because I was pregnant, and I was able to handle the load as much as I could and I was comfortable doing so.

I had lots of energy, and I was able to do my job. I worked until I was thirty-seven weeks pregnant. Das was born in August 2018, four days after our sixth wedding anniversary. I took a twelve-week maternity leave. When I went back to work, I continued to bond with my patients. They even bonded with me. I really liked the job and the patients.

In January 2019, I took my hemodialysis certification exam and passed. I knew my job well enough to continue providing patient care. In July 2019, I found out I was pregnant with my third baby boy. Malik is affectionately known as Max or Leek. He was definitely my surprise baby. I didn't know I was pregnant for six weeks. I worked until thirty-eight weeks. I stayed light on my feet, took breaks as needed, and was full of energy. My patients made sure I wasn't working too hard, and they were very supportive during my pregnancy.

This career has been one of the most rewarding experiences. I have learned the ropes, and one of the most rewarding opportunities is that I get a chance to help people receive their dialysis treatment safely and properly.

I have grown to love and care for strangers because I've learned that a smile and kindness can go a long way in helping patients get through some rough times in their lives. I help them learn more about their treatments. Whether I cannulate this patient or that patient—or not—I'm glad to be able to make a difference in their lives. I have learned so much from my patients about health, illness, and the journey life takes us on.

CHAPTER 2

Hypertension: Dietary and Lifestyle Factors

I'm a devoted wife and mother to three handsome and intelligent young sons. My life is very busy and fulfilling as the only queen and female energy in our home. It is so precious. I appreciate, love and cherish my family, and I'm so blessed to have them in my life.

I chose to write this book based on my personal experiences with hypertension and disease in my family. I want to share my experience as a Certified Clinical Hemodialysis Technician and my concerns, views, and solutions about the alarming rise in men and women between twenty and fifty who are on dialysis because of hypertension (high blood pressure). Chronic kidney failure and hypertension are directly related to hemodialysis among this age group. Other factors such as chronic illnesses and preexisting conditions like diabetes play a big role too, but hypertension is rampant. It can cause a person who seems healthy to quickly become a dialysis patient.

Hypertension is a preventable condition that can be treated quickly and effectively before it damages the blood and delicate organs. Most of the people who end up on dialysis didn't even know their kidneys were shutting down. They had the silent, asymptomatic signs of high blood pressure, and when their kidneys "went to sleep" or became dormant, the individual requires dialysis. Their worlds are turned upside down, and not enough voices are speaking out about our health as a community and a nation.

Imagine your whole life, good and bad memories, past and present experiences, triumphs, and tragedies, every fiber of your entire existence, and your blood all being circulated, refreshed, cleaned, and renewed inside a machine. An artificial kidney is performing daily essential functions your biological kidney would naturally perform without the assistance of a machine. This is the life of a dialysis patient, three days a week, ranging from three to five hours of treatment. A dialyzer acts as the kidney by removing excess fluids and toxins from the body to keep a person alive. Many patients live normal, everyday lives while adapting to their new abnormal lives. I call it "life in a machine." Your body is dependent on a machine instead of itself for survival; without dialysis, it's a life-or-death situation. You cannot live without your kidneys. You cannot ditch dialysis if your kidneys are partially working or not working at all. Dialysis doesn't necessarily the end of your life or the world you exist in.

In this book, my main objective is to discuss hypertension (high blood pressure), kidney function and abnormalities, and nutrition. Hypertension is growing and having a big impact on young old Asiatic individuals in America. "Asiatic" is what society calls black or brown people. In science, black means death. When the living tissues in a human being die, they become necrotic and black. In *Black's Law Dictionary.* there is no such thing as those described brands. We are Moors, the original inhabitants of America, and for the context of this book, I address and properly recognize those referred to as "Black people" as Asiatic Moors.

> Black as adjective (adj.) Old English blaec absolutely dark, absorbing all light, the color of soot or coal from Proto Germanic blakaz burned (source also of Old Norse blakkr dark," Old high German blah "black, Swedish black "ink," Dutch blaken "to burn"), from PIE bhleg. To burn gleam. Shine, flash" (source also of Greek phlegein to burn, scorch, Latin flagrare to blaze glow, burn), from root bhel.1 to shine, flash or burn.

The same root produced Old English blac "bright, shining, glittering pale, the connecting notions being, perhaps, fire bright and burned" dark or perhaps absence of color. There is nothing more variable than the signification of words designating colour. Hensleigh Wedgwood, A dictionary of English Etymology (1859) (Online Etymology Dictionary).

Act 6- With us all members must proclaim their Nationality and we are teaching our people their Nationality and their Divine Creed that they must know that they are part and parcel of this Said Government, and know that they are not Negroes, Colored, Folks, Black People or Ethiopians, because these names were given to slaves by slave holders in 1779 and lasted until 1865 during the time of slavery, but this is a new era of time now, and all men now must proclaim their free national name to be recognized by the government in which they live and the nations of the earth, this is the reason why Allah the Great God of the Universe ordained Noble Drew Ali, the Prophet to redeem his people from their sinful ways. The Moorish Americans are the descendants of the Ancient Moabites whom inhabited the northwestern and southwestern shores of Africa. (The Naturalization Orientation Book)

Approximately 99 percent of the dialysis patients in my unit are Asiatic Moors between the ages of twenty and fifty. High blood pressure, kidney failure, and dietary lifestyle play major roles in the deterioration of Asiatics' kidney functions. Kidney disease was once viewed as an older individual's disease, but it is showing up without warning in younger Asiatics in our communities. I felt a need to sound the alarm about what's happening with so many of our Asiatic brothers and sisters. I will provide some insight into what we need to do as a community. This disease can be eradicated with healthier and more balanced lifestyles.

It's amazing how many of our people are on these machines. I believe Asiatic Moors are sensitive to acidic foods and the lifestyles that they have been adapting to for hundreds of years. Society tells us that hypertension is the number one killer of Moors. It is genetic, and if your grandparents and parents had the disease, it will be passed down to you and your children. It is passed down from generation to generation because many Asiatics enjoy traditional, southern, fried, down-home cooking. These comfort foods have created chronic diseases that harm our blood pressure and vital organs, especially our kidneys.

The traditional health and diet choices have failed our people. It is not enough to just say that high blood pressure runs in the family and we are all going to get it. It is also not enough to just say that hypertension is the number one killer in our communities. That is nothing to be proud of. If we do not let go of traditions that have never served our communities, they were never our traditions to begin with. We are burying our people younger and younger because we don't want to give up the very thing that is killing us. People know it is wrong, but it feels so right! You can change certain things to enhance and improve your life.

Our nation has failed us. There is too much obesity, chronic disease, and hypertension. The food manufacturers in this country determine what our families consume at the dinner table. People have been misinformed about what's good for them. For example, pork is very harmful for our bodies, but commercials call pork "the other white meat." They claim that it is nutritious and a good source of protein. That animal is filthy, and it eats slop and anything else you feed it. It rolls around in its own waste and mud, and it is very lazy. Americans consume this animal like it's the best meat ever eaten. Pork by-products are in toothpaste, gum, some fruit juices, and Jell-o and gelatin products. Why is pork in products that are used by people? Even in dialysis, the heparin medicine that prevents the blood from clotting is a pork by-product.

Pork clogs the arteries in the heart. Animal fats and animal by-products can clog the arteries and vessels. This prevents blood flow to the heart and other vital organs. The arteries and blood vessels harden, which restricts blood flow and raises blood pressure. Some patients have chronic hypertension, which means they have consistent high blood pressure. Their systolic pressure is always over 180 mmg, and their diastolic pressure is always over 100 mmg. That is very dangerous, and patients with this condition risk heart attacks, strokes, seizures, kidney failure, paralysis, and even death. Some patients are ignorant about how high blood pressure affects their lives during dialysis treatments, and some are not. Some of their diets and lifestyles are definitely contributing factors, some patients are defiant and on dialysis, and some patients are barely holding on to life.

> For the life of the flesh is in the blood, and I have given it to you upon the altar to make an atonement for your souls: for it is the blood that maketh an atonement for the soul! (Leviticus 17:11)

Your blood is your life! Your blood is the umbilical cord to life and its wonderful, mysterious creations. Life begins and ends with your blood! Blood is responsible for all of life's creations. It is needed for every interaction within the body's circulatory, hormonal, and endocrinal systems. It affects brain function and every nerve impulse. We need blood like water, and blood is made up of 90 percent of water.

> Normal blood pH is the measurement of the free hydrogen ions that can be released to other substances Acid is measured by pH on a scale 0-6.9 acidic, 7 is neutral 7.01- 14 is (alkaline). Normal arterial blood is 7.35 − 7.45. (Greenfield Health Systems)(Green book) is the most vital and essential unique, nutrient dense, transports fluid and responsible for blood acid, base and electrolytes in the human body. Blood begins with all of life's creations, its red, crimson tide has powerful yet millions and trillions of red blood cells, white blood cells and platelets, responsible for homeostatic properties that helps balance vital, multi- organ systems 24 hours a day 7 days a week by the seconds. Red blood cells consists of blood, Co2, white blood cells, platelets, plasma protein

and metabolic wastes, among other health properties. (Greenfield Health Systems Green Book)

However blood and its life sustaining properties in organ systems in the body through blood pressure. Blood pressure is regulated through the arterial walls within the cardiovascular system. BP= CO cardiac output xPR Peripheral resistance. The mmHg means millimeters of mercury which were used in the first accurate mercury pressure gauges still used in modern medicine. The viscosity venous return the standard unit rate and force of heart contractions and the elasticity of the arteries. (*Pathophysiology for the Health Professions*, fourth edition, 280)

Blood pressure depends on cardiac output and peripheral resistance. Specific variables include blood volume, Systolic- pressure is determined by the higher number is exerted by the blood when ejected from the left ventricle of the heart. (*Pathophysiology for the Health Professions*, Fourth Edition, 280)

Diastolic pressure is the lower value, which means the pressure sustained when the ventricles are relaxed or rested.

The American Heart Association has displayed blood pressure categories:

Normal- Systolic mmHg (upper number) is less than 120 Diastolic mmHg (lower number) less than 80.

High blood pressure (Hypertension Stage 1) Systolic pressure (130–139) Diastolic 80–89.

High Blood Pressure (Hypertension Stage 2) Systolic 140 or higher Diastolic 90 or higher.

Hypertensive Crisis (consult a doctor immediately) Systolic – 180 or higher Diastolic Higher than 120.

When blood pressure is involved, there is no denying how heart rate goes hand and hand. Heart rate is the number of times the heart beats per minute, so just because your heart rate increases doesn't mean your blood pressure will at the same time. (American Heart Association.org)

Blood pressure is elevated by increased SNS stimulation in the rain and nervous system.

1 SNS and epinephrine act at the beta adrenergic receptors in the heart to increase both the rate and force of contraction.

2. SNS epinephrine and non-epinephrine increase vasoconstriction by stimulating the alpha receptors in the arterioles of the skin and viscera. This reduces the capacity of the system and increase venous return.

Other hormones contribute to control of blood pressure, antidiuretic hormone (ADH) increases water reabsorption through the kidney, thus increasing blood, volume ADH also known vasocontraction.

Aldosterone increases blood volume by increasing reabsorption of sodium, ions, and water. Also the renin angiotensin, aldosterone system in the kidneys is an important control and compensation mechanism that is initiated when there is any decrease renal blood flow. (Greenfield Health Systems Green Book)

All of our organs are connected to one another. The benefits and damages have domino effects. The body and its organ systems are like a roadway; one road of blood and fluid leads to the next destination and vice versa. All arteries, veins, and transport systems make up human beings. Our blood is everything, and everything we are made up of is blood. In the creation of life, a male sperm is made up of blood, and a woman has a menstrual cycle every month. The uterus and its nutrient-rich blood environment create a safe space for babies to grow.

> Fluid and Electrolyte Balance plays a vital role with blood pressure as well. Electrolytes are positive and negative ions that create an electrical current. Functions of Electrolytes are Sodium, Calcium, Bicarbonate (HCO3-) Phosphates (PO4) Magnesium, Albumin, Potassium and Blood Urea Nitrogen, Creatinine. (Greenfield Health Systems Green Book)

Low blood pressure can be just as harmful to the body because not enough oxygen is being delivered to the multi-organ systems. Without enough oxygen, the multi- organ systems cannot function properly, leaving them deprived of nutrients and other life-sustaining properties, ultimately leading to death.

High blood pressure (hypertension) is detrimental to the blood. High and low blood pressure are both important. Low blood pressure can be dangerous because not enough oxygen is being distributed to vital organs. A patient's blood pressure can drop so low that they pass out and never wake up. They can be extremely anemic, always feel cold, and have low iron, blue lips, blue or black fingertips or toes, discoloration of nails, poor circulation, and amputated extremities. Low blood pressure can be dangerous and deadly.

Blood pressure has a direct impact on the kidneys. The kidneys are two bean-shaped organs that sit retroperitoneal in the abdominal cavity (*Pathophysiology for the Health Professions*, 440) The kidneys are covered by a fibrous capsule and are embedded in fat with the superior portion also protected by the lower ribs (*Pathophysiology for the Health Professions*, 440).

> Inside each kidney is the cortex, or outer layer in which the majority of the glomeruli are located, and

the medulla or inner section of the tissue which consists primarily of the medulla lie in the renal pelvis and calyces, through which urine flows in the ureter. Each kidney consists of over a million nephrons, the functional units of the kidney. The renal corpuscle consists of Bowman capsule glomerular capsule which is the blind end of the proximal convoluted tubule. This capsule surrounds a network of capillaries called the glomerulus capillaries.

The Renal anatomy also includes:

Ureters: a pair of mucosa lined, transports urine from renal pelvis to the bladder.

Urinary bladder: a mucosal pouch located in the pelvis.

Urethra: the tube that conveys urine from the bladder to the urinary meatus for excretion.

During filtration a large volume of fluid, including wastes, nutrients, electrolytes, and other dissolved substances, passes from the blood into the tubule cells and protein remain in the blood. When filtration pressure increases more filtrate flows into the tubule consists of three parts, the proximal convoluted tubule, the loop of henle and the distal convoluted tubule.

Functions of the kidney:

Electrolyte and Acid base balance, sodium, calcium, potassium, and phosphorus.

Metabolic waste Elimination BUN and Creatinine.

Control of fluid balance.

Hormone Influence:

Erythropoietin RBCS (red blood cells)

Vitamin D- Enhances intestinal absorption.

Parathyroid glands- 4 small glands secretes of parathyroid hormone.

Posterior pituitary gland- Secretions of antidiuretic hormone.

Adrenal gland- is stimulated to release aldosterone thus by vasoconstriction and H20 and Na+ retention.

Blood pressure is closely related to kidney function and frequently it is elevated with renal aka, kidney disease. When the blood flow or blood pressure in the afferent arteriole decreases for any reason, the renin angiotensin aldosterone triad is stimulated. Angiotensin not only causes systemic vasoconstriction it also stimulates the secretion of aldosterone. This hormone increases blood volume, thus increasing blood pressure serum renin levels which can determine whether this mechanism is a factor in hypertension (high blood pressure). In which case renin blocking drugs can be prescribed. (Greenfield Health Systems Green Book)

The kidneys are very important to the body. They are responsible for so much of our blood pressure and hormones. We definitely need them to sustain removal of waste from the body. It's amazing how you can take urination every day for granted. However, the kidney function can be disrupted due to disease and various imbalances that may occur.

These disruptions fall into 3 categories of Kidney Disease:

Pre-Renal: decreased blood flow to the kidney Ex: Burns, Sepsis, shock hypovolemia, low cardiac output.

Intra renal: damage to the kidney Ex: Crush syndrome, nephrotoxic substance, toxemia.

Post Renal: Blocking flow from the kidney Ex: Tumors, stones, Prostate hypertrophy, surgical litigation.

The first type of kidney/ or renal failure is called Acute Renal Failure (ARF) or Acute Kidney Injury (AKI). This is caused by a severe impairment or shutdown of the renal function, its usually reversible this condition lasts for a few weeks to a few months, kidneys function can resume on its own. Examples of AKI are kidney stones, alcohol poisoning, car, bike accident or pre/ post injury.

Chronic Kidney Disease (CKD) or End Stage Renal Disease (ESRD) Most people have chronic kidney disease from Diabetes or Hypertension. Also pyelonephritis, inflammation of the kidney caused by E.coli infection, congenital disorder, auto immune infection, and polycystic kidney disease (inflammation of the glomerulus or strep infection It is a slow progressive loss or renal function, damage persisting over 3 months. Treatment goals usually are slow progression, support body function, provide psychosocial support and educate patients regarding treatment choices.

There are 5 stages to CKD: Kidney disease is based on the presence of kidney damage and the glomerular filtration rate (GFR) which is a measure of your level, of kidney function. Treatment is based on the stage of kidney disease. (National Kidney Foundation, Nutrition and Early Kidney Disease Are you getting what you need ? (Stage 1–4)

Stage 1: Kidney Damage (Protein in the urine, with normal (GFR) 90 or above.

Stage 2: Kidney damage with mild decrease in (GFR) 60 to 89

Stage 3: Kidney damage with moderate decrease in (GFR) 30 to 59

Stage 4: Kidney damage severe reduction in (GFR) 15 to 29

Stage 5: Kidney failure (GFR) less than 15 (Greenfield Health Systems Greenbook)

A person's urine can tell them when they are having problems with the kidneys. With kidney stones and gallbladder issues, salts and other elements in the body create crystalline rocks in the urine, which causes moderate to extreme pain when passing through the narrow urethra. Ouch! Holding urine for long periods of time can affect blood pressure! When I had my son, I had some urinary incontinence. The nurse saw that my blood pressure was elevated, but she told me to go to the restroom to relieve myself—and my blood pressure went down after a while.

Dialysis patients who still produce urine need to go to the restroom during dialysis if their blood pressure is too high. If a patient needs to urinate and comes back to continue their treatment, their blood pressure sometimes won't be as high. A patient may see a rise in blood pressure if they are rushing to receive their treatment. Everything affects blood pressure!

Wow! The kidneys needs to release the buildup of waste, toxins, and urea, and not doing so in a timely matter disrupts normal and healthy bacteria in the kidney, bladder, and urethra. This can cause infection and inflammation and eventually impairs the normal function of those organs. Some of these effects can result in strong antibiotics, urinary incontinence, or uncontrollable bladder issues.

Without proper function of the kidneys, blood pressure can remain out of sync for long periods of time, which definitely causes disruptions within the body. A person can live a healthy life with only one healthy kidney. Many dialysis patients are on the kidney transplant list. A patient normally waits three to five years to receive a kidney transplant, but the patient must come to dialysis treatment every time they are scheduled. They must follow the suggested renal diets, and their blood results should remain in good standing with phosphorus, potassium, and calcium levels within normal ranges.

Kidney transplants aren't as easy as they seem. The treatments go beyond the patient. Dialysis social workers have to know that patients have the mental stability to go back to their normal pre-dialysis life with the support of their families during the transition.

Some patients are wary about all of the antirejection kidney medication and steroids that they would be on after the transplant. They wonder if it's really worth taking all that medicine and risking their lives just to stay alive. Some patients don't want transplants, especially older patients. They feel like they lived their lives, and if they are meant to die in old age, then that's what Allah wants. They think nothing is going to wake up their kidneys, and they don't want to go to dialysis three times a week. Some patients' kidneys are damaged beyond repair, and they must get their health in order to receive a kidney transplant—even if they are older than sixty-five.

Some dialysis patients look forward to coming to dialysis to get away from abusive or unstable issues in their homes. Some patients are able to get their best sleep on the machines because they cannot sleep well at home. If they live alone, they may come to dialysis to have someone to talk to—whether it's other patients, dialysis technicians, or nurses.

Treating dialysis patients with compassion and kindness can give them hope and make their days—even it's only for a few minutes. I'm honored to do so for my patients. I speak with patients from other units, and I give them the same treatment as if they were patients at West Pavilion Dialysis unit.

CHAPTER 3

Hemodialysis: A Day in the life of a Dialysis patient

Dialysis provides an artificial kidney which can be used to sustain life after the kidneys fail.

> There is considerable reserve in the renal system; an individual can function normally with half of one kidney. Dialysis is used to treat someone who has acute renal failure, perhaps until a transplant becomes available. (*Pathophysiology for the Health Professions*, 448)

There are two forms of dialysis: peritoneal dialysis and hemodialysis. Hemodialysis is provided in a hospital, dialysis center, or at home with special equipment and training. During the procedure, the patient's blood moves from an implanted shunt or catheter in an artery, often in the arm, through a tube to a machine where the exchange of wastes, fluids, and electrolytes takes place. A semipermeable membrane separates the patient's blood from the dialysis fluid (dialysate) and the constituents move between the two compartments. For example, wastes move from blood to the dialysate while bicarbonate ion moves into the blood from the dialysate.

Blood cells and protein remain in the blood, unable to pass through the semi- permeable membrane. Movement of Ultrafiltration, diffusion (by concentration gradient), and osmosis. After the exchange has been completed, the blood is returned to the patient's vein. Heparin or another anticoagulant is administer to prevent clotting, requiring monitoring of blood clotting times. The session because fluid and electrolyte balances change quickly, but usually he or she feels better after treatment. The feeling of well0being then dissipates gradually as wastes accumulate before the next treatment.

Dialysis has potential complications. The shunt may become infected, or blood clots may form. Eventually the blood vessels involved at the shunt becomes sclerosed or damaged and a new site must be selected. Patients on dialysis have an increased risk of infection by the hepatitis B or C viruses or human immunodeficiency virus (HIV).

Hemodialysis is usually required three times a week, each session lasting about 3 to 4 hours and up to 5 hours for some patients. The patient may feel uncomfortable during the treatment (*Pathophysiology for the Health Professions*, 448)

Blood pressure plays a very vital role in sustaining life and vitality to the body. It can create blood disturbances that damage the organ systems, especially the kidneys, heart, and brain. We need blood pressure to remain balanced in every waking moment, and there is not enough discussion to really focus on how important blood pressure is for the blood. For hemodialysis patients, it can keep patients stable or unstable, creating a very dangerous situation for the patient and staff members.

Blood pressure plays a part in a patient's dialysis treatment, and do arterial pressure and venous pressure. These deal with the pressures for blood going in and out of the body for cleansing of the blood. The arterial pressure is responsible for the pressure of the blood from the arterial artery during treatment:

> Both hypertension (HTN) and CKD are serious interrelated global public health problems. Nearly 30 percent and 15 percent of US adults have HTN and CKD respectively. Because HTN may cause or result from CKD HTN prevalence is higher and control more difficult with worse kidney function. Etiology of CKD, presence and degree of albuminuria, and genetic factors all influence HTN severity and prevalence. In addition, socioeconomic and lifestyle factors influence HTN prevalence and control. There are racial and ethnic disparities in the prevalence, treatment, risks, and outcomes of HTN in patients with CKD. Control of blood pressure (BP) in Hispanic and African Americans with CKD is worse than whites. There are disparities in the patterns of treatment and rates of progression of CKD in patients with HTN. The presence and severity of CKD increase treatment resistance. HTN is also extremely prevalent in patients receiving hemodialysis, and optimal targets for BP control of HTN in CKD patients is improving, control of BP in patients at all stages of CKD remains suboptimal. (Bruce Horowitz, Dana Miskulin, Philip Zager, "Epidemiology of hypertension in CKD," *Adv Chronic Kidney Dis.* March 2015, 22(2):88–95. doi: 10.1053/j.ackd.2014.09.004)

Some patients have been on dialysis for twenty or thirty years, and they are still thriving and living their best lives. The first patient I ever saw having dialysis was my mother. I was studying for a science degree, and I wanted to become a nurse or have a career in the medical field. My mother was a lab technician for more than twenty years, and I wanted to follow in her footsteps. She unexpectedly became very ill with stage 5 kidney disease, heart disease, and hypertension, and she received inpatient dialysis treatment. The hypertension drastically affected her organs, especially her kidneys.

My mother received dialysis via an internal jugular catheter port, but I really didn't understand the process. All I knew was that it was prolonging her life for however long she had remaining to live. I will never forget seeing my mother on dialysis. Her blood, the crimson tide of life and memories, was spinning around and around to keep her alive. I didn't think of becoming a dialysis technician, and it never crossed my mind to go into that field of work. I couldn't imagine everything she was feeling and going through mentally. I know it was physically draining. It was depressing for us both, and I knew from her facial expressions and the severity of her illness that it was very uncomfortable. I saw how serious this disease was, and I knew it could happen to me if I wasn't careful with my own health. I took it as a warning, but some other family members didn't.

My mother had been on dialysis for seven months when her life was cut short due to complications of her kidney disease. It was five days after my twenty-fourth birthday in 2010. The sadness and pain took me to a dark place. That empty feeling and the void in my life will never be filled.

I still see and feel my mother's presence in my children, which reminds me that she is still here with us in spirit. I know that she would have been very proud of me following in her footsteps and helping others with the illnesses she experienced. I have the energy and willpower to continue the lessons and blessings bestowed upon me to help others.

This experience has definitely been a lesson. It's not easy to see people, especially the younger generation, in the fight for their lives. Kidney disease is moving through our society at a high speed, and it's other cultures and races are being affected by it too. Individuals in their twenties, thirties, forties and fifties are experiencing kidney damage, which was once considered an elderly person's disease.

A person doesn't have to drink massive amounts of water to keep their kidneys healthy, Kidney health goes beyond water and types of water, including alkaline or purified water. Kidney health is about overall nutrition, stress management, rest and sleep, mental health, and exercise.

A typical dialysis patient's diet and fluid, sodium, phosphorus, and other blood levels intake definitely play a role in dialysis treatment. Dietitians play a vital role in assisting patients with renal diets. According to the pamphlet Greenfield Health Systems called "Fluids During the Summer," anything that pours, melts, or is liquid at room temperature is a fluid. Fluids are what you drink and the foods you eat, including alcohol, salt-free broths, soups, coffee, tea, cream, milk, nondairy creamer, gelatin, ice cream, popsicles, juice, lemonade, nutritional drinks, pop, soda, shakes, sherbet, sorbet, water, and watermelon.

> There is a limit to how much can be safely removed during a dialysis treatment, fluid limits will vary among patients. Too much fluid causes: Swelling, shortness of breath, fluid in the lungs, and around your heart, high blood pressure, heart failure cramping and other difficulties, during dialysis, hospitalization. Avoiding salty, sweet foods can limit the strong urge to drink.

A renal diet can be a more restrictive than what a person was used to before dialysis. Not all patients follow the restrictive diet that helps during dialysis. Many patients continue their unhealthy eating habits, including fried, salty, sweet, sugary foods, alcohol, soda, and recreational drugs. Their mindset is that they're going to be on dialysis for the rest of their lives, and they might as well do as they please while they're still alive. Some patients take their health seriously and want to survive and get off of dialysis. These patients watch their fluid intake, watch what they eat, exercise, and try to maintain a normal life to get on the transplant list to receive a kidney.

A lot of patients deal with mood swings, including depression, loss of appetite, weight loss, and weight gain. They can get ill from all the toxins that build up in their bodies. Their tissues swell, and they need to be hospitalized. Others pass away from other comorbidities. Some patients experience job loss because of the side effects of getting dialysis treatment three times a week. They can't keep up with the everyday demands of employment. Some receive social security, disability payments, or other governmental benefits. In extreme cases, they are suicidal or stop going to their dialysis treatments.

Some patients are on dialysis for a few years, and if their bodies cannot handle the dialysis, they die. Dialysis brings so many emotional, mental, physical, and spiritual issues to patients and their families. If the kidneys won't do their jobs, the machine does it for them. All of your blood, which is your, life is literally inside the machine. Some patients suffer from blood clots during dialysis. Blood thinners can cause excessive bleeding when the needles are removed from the graft or fistula site. It is truly a blessing to be able to do normal human things like go to the bathroom to urinate after drinking a favorite beverage. Otherwise, the fluids build up in the body, which makes the patient feel terrible and full until their next dialysis treatment.

When people with compromised immune systems, sexually transmitted diseases or infections, including herpes, HIV, AIDS, and syphilis, become dialysis patients, the medications can damages their kidneys. Dealing with more than one disease at a time makes life more complicated and more complex.

Cancer patients have different issues that affect their kidneys when they receive chemotherapy and dialysis. It seem unfair, but there is a light at the end of the tunnel. It is a bumpy road, and they need strength and courage to heal. Otherwise, the illness can take them down a grim road they never return from.

> Cardiovascular (CV) disease is the leading cause of morbidity and mortality in the United States end stage renal disease (ESRD) population. Annually, approximately 30 percent of hospitalizations and 50 percent of deaths are attributed to CV causes. The etiology of CV disease among individuals receiving maintenance hemodialysis differs from that of the general population. Dialysis specific risk factors such as repeated, large intradialytic fluid, and blood

pressure (BP) shifts likely play substantial pathological roles in dialysis- associated CV risk. Typical systolic BP decline in characterized by 2 phases, a relatively rapid BP decline in the first quarter of the treatment followed by a more gradual BP decline in the latter 75 percent of treatment. Deviations from the typical BP course such as intradialytic hypotension (a precipitous BP drop during hemodialysis and intradialytic hypertension (a paradoxical pre dialysis to post dialysis BP rise also known as post dialysis hypertension) have been associated with increased morbidity and mortality. Of the 2 BP abnormalities, intradialytic hypertension has received comparatively less attention.

During dialysis treatments patients do experience high blood pressure called intradialytic hypertension. Intradialytic hypertension is an increase in blood pressure from pre to post hemodialysis that has recently been identified as an independent mortality risk in hypertension have been explored in numerous research studies over the past few years.

Patients with intradialytic hypertension have been found to be more chronically volume overloaded compared to other hemodialysis patients, although no casual role has been established. Patients with intradialytic hypertension have intradialytic vascular resistance surges that likely explain the blood pressure increase during dialysis. Acute intradialytic changes in endothelial cell function have been proposed as etiologies for the increase in vascular resistance is an association between dialysate to serum sodium gradients and blood pressure increase during dialysis in patients with intradialytic hypertension, although it is unclear if this is related to endothelial cell activity or acute osmolar changes.

In addition to probing the dry weight of patients with intradialytic hypertension other management strategies include lowering dialysate sodium and changing antihypertensives to include carvedilol or other poorly dialyzed antihypertensives.

Hemodialysis patients with intradialytic hypertension have an increased mortality risk compared to patients with modest decreases in blood pressure during dialysis. Intradialytic hypertension is associated with extracellular volume overload in addition to acute increases in vascular resistance during dialysis. Management strategies should include reevaluation of dry weight and modification of both the dialysate prescription and medication prescription. (*Mechanisms and Treatment of Intradialytic Hypertension*, Peter Noel Van Buren MD, MSCS and Julia K Inrig, MD MHS University of Texas Southwestern Medical Center, Department of Internal Medicine and Division of Nephrology, Duke University Medical Center, Department of Internal Medicine, Division of Nephrology, Therapeutic Science and Strategy Unit, Quintiles Clinical Research Organization)

CHAPTER 4

A Balanced Dietary Lifestyle

To keep blood pressure in a normal range, it is important to eat a balanced and alkaline diet. A balanced and alkaline diet includes natural, low-acidic foods that work in conjunction for proper nutrient absorption in the body. It doesn't disrupt the blood pressure and cell rejuvenation, and it restores health in body functions. Nutrient foods are organic, seeded fruits and vegetables from the earth (non-GMO, unseeded, lab-grown foods). Beans and legumes are good for iron absorption. Grains and wild black rice include vitamins A, C, E, and K and minerals like potassium, magnesium, chromium, selenium, and iron. Many other minerals are vital for everyday cell rejuvenation, which brings life to the body. Alkaline water is a great source of liquid hydration, which the body needs on a daily basis. Buying alkaline water on the pH scale of seven to ten gives the body total hydration and keeps blood pressure stable. Consuming half a gallon to a gallon a day is vital for blood and is a great flush for the kidneys.

More than 661,000 Americans have kidney failure, 468,000 individuals are on dialysis, and 193,000 live with a functioning kidney transplant. Kidney disease often has no symptoms in its early stages and can go undetected until it is very advanced. It has been estimated that thirty-seven million American adults have chronic kidney disease (CKD). CKD has two main causes: high blood pressure and diabetes. If undetected, CKD can progress to irreversible kidney failure. People with kidney failure require dialysis or a kidney transplant to live. Minority populations, particularly African Americans, Hispanics and Latinos, Native Americans, and Alaska Natives suffer disproportionate rates of CKD and kidney failure.

The blood is the ultimate climate for balance and sustainability in the human body. There are also environmental and external factors that create disturbances to blood pressure in the American, Westernized diet, including high-fat foods, acidic diets, alcohol, and obesity. The biggest contributing factors for high blood pressure disturbances create disease and chronic health conditions such as diabetes, stroke, heart disease, and kidney failure.

We live in a fast-paced, on-the-go society with our careers, social media, microwaveable processed food, lack of sleep, improper hydration, and sleep deprivation.

The Asiatic community suffers from the fatal blow of high blood pressure. Hypertension is the number one killer and disease for Asiatics. The old slave diet or the infamous soul food is also known as comfort food, which we enjoy every Sunday for dinner and the traditional pagan holidays. As slaves in the southern states, Asiatic Moors protein came from the flesh of pigs, cows, and various animals. Asiatic Moors wore it like a badge of honor, and that remains true for some to this day. We were able to create all types of fried, fattening, and delicious cuisines, and the recipes were passed down through the generations. Diets included bacon, eggs, chitlings, ham hocks, pork, ribs, beef oxtails, macaroni and cheese, fried chicken, collard greens cooked with pieces of pork, and assorted cakes and pies prepared with a lot of white sugar, salt, and animal products, including eggs, butter, and milk. Unfortunately, soul food and traditional southern recipes have created a lot of problems for our communities.

A lot of greasy, salty animal flesh foods are acidic, which means they disrupt the cells and natural processes for proper nutritional absorption in the body. The grease and animal fats clog the arteries and various blood vessels of the heart (arthrosclerosis), gallbladder (gallstones) kidneys (kidney stones), and liver (fatty liver disease). Dairy products, such as cheese, eggs, and milk create a mucus film of secretions in the stomach lining and respiratory tract. Disruptions such as lactose intolerance and digestive issues clog these areas for normal bowel movements and function.

Beef products such as steak, oxtails, and other red meat can take up to a week to digest in the colon tract. The small and large intestine have to get rid of the beef products through this long process. This is taxing on the body since it cannot fully digest the meat, which causes abdominal bloating, gas, constipation, hard stools, upset stomach, moodiness, and lack of sleep, which the body needs to rejuvenate itself. Blood pressure becomes elevated because the body is out of the homeostatic cycle that brings healthy blood flow to arteries, veins, and blood vessels. Continued and uncontrolled high blood pressure damages arteries, veins, and blood vessels. They become weak and thin, making it difficult to keep vital organs healthy. The lack of blood flow builds up toxins, mucus, and disease—and eventually organ failure.

Sunday dinners and pagan holidays were like national holidays in my family. All the mothers, fathers, grandmas, grandpas, aunties, uncles, cousins, and close family friends would get together to talk smack, laugh, and reminisce. We would eat big meals, gain weight, and get sleepy. We would eat, nap, wake up, and eat some more. The meals were golden and were treated like rites of passage. They were only prepared by the best cooks in the family. We would have fried chicken, barbeque pork ribs, hot dogs, hot sausages, hamburgers, steaks, starchy pastas, macaroni and cheese, hamburger spaghetti, pasta salad, collard greens, green string beans with pork fat and seasonings, sweet cakes and pies, soda pop, and alcoholic beverages for the adults.

I remember growing up with my family and eating these traditional meals.I remember elders would say, "You will become big and strong by eating all your meat and milk." "This food sticks to your ribs, and this is real good eating."

The aftereffects of eating this food was an overstuffed, full feeling, indigestion, constipation, and the ultimate gluttonous behavior of eating more until you fell into a food coma. When I became older, those statements couldn't have been further from the truth. Although the meals brought our family and other Asiatic families together, they also tore us apart through sickness, disease, and death. I always wondered how this food we consumed, which was supposed to be so good for us, would eventually kill us. Older and younger family members lost their lives to diabetes, heart disease, and kidney failure. The generational chain of sickness and disease continued in my family.

As a young girl, I ate a lot of salty and sugary snacks, but the ingredients in those snacks and foods were different. I was very physically active, which burned a lot of calories. Weight gain and a sedentary lifestyle were not something I experienced. Some children were overweight and had sedentary childhoods. They stayed in their houses eating junk food and playing video games. Most children were riding bikes, playing tag and hide-and-seek, and playing with friends. The children would play outside until the streetlights came on.

Babies eat pureed fruits and vegetables because they are nutritional and easier to digest. Doctors suggest not giving babies meat because it is not digestible for a baby, and it can hurt their stomachs. What do you think meat does to an adult's body? Consuming large quantities of meat makes it hard for our bodies to digest it!

Asiatic people are dying off very fast because of the silent killer. Hypertension is called the silent killer because most people who have hypertension do not have the symptoms associated with high blood pressure. The classic symptoms are dizziness, a funny weak feeling, and severe headaches. We don't want to give up the acidic foods that are considered traditional and taste good. Whatever Grandma said about food is true, yet the grandmothers in our communities were battling her own diseases in silence, trying to feed their families, and keeping traditions alive. Grandmothers had diabetes or the "sugars" as they would call it. They were losing toes, fingers, and limbs, but they refused to stop baking cakes with pounds of sugar, salt, and butter.

There are medical issues with the pancreas and insulin production and cortisol levels in the brain that can cause diabetes. The older generations didn't know about proper diet and health, and the ones who knew were looked down upon with statements that you need these heavy foods to stick to your ribs, you were not meant to be skinny, and you cannot survive on only fruits and vegetables. Asiatic people didn't know any better, and some of them were too stuck in their own ways to eat better, which is still the case for some of them today.

Hope is not lost because of the stigma that plagues our communities, but in our communities, the grocery stores aren't selling fresh organic fruits and vegetables. Some are starting to provide fresh produce through gardens and farmers markets. They are selling cheap manager's specials on groceries that are too old and not edible the next day. They are making consumers sick with food poisoning and other food-related illnesses. However, more farmers markets are popping up in urban communities with local gardens and healthy eating for families.

Asiatics' bodies are very sensitive to the dangerous effects of how hypertension is blowing the kidney functions out. Blood pressure is elevated to maximum levels, and kidney function is minimized or diminished. The food chain is brewing with all types of processed food, salt- and sugar-filled snacks, chips, and candies. Even children are being diagnosed with type 2 diabetes, high blood pressure, and kidney problems. Sugary beverages like juice and pop are hurting their tender organs when their bodies haven't even had time to grow well with a healthy diet. Younger Asiatics are being greatly affected by this disease, but some of them are starting to take better control and research the food system and how it affects their bodies. The generational chain needs to be broken and reconstructed immediately! It can be done hypertension isn't the end-all, be-all for better health and blood pressure numbers.

Many Asiatic families don't understand how these foods have made our families very ill and killed a lot of them. Asiatics have believed that since our ancestors ate foods like this, we should continue consuming these foods. Our ancestors ate lots of fruits and vegetables. They grew their own food and made their own herbal medicines and healing remedies for healthy living. They even had their own businesses, commerce, language, and religion, which was originally Islam! There are Hebrew Moslems living in Northwest Africa, which is what we now call America.

Western history books and articles taught us that we came from Africa as slaves on a boat and migrated to North America, residing predominately in the southern states. The truth of the matter is not every Asiatic was bought over to North America. We were already here with our own land, customs, businesses, and religion. Centuries ago Asiatic people grew their own food and were not meat eaters. They consumed fruits, vegetables, plants and herbs.

Meat was not introduced to the North American shores until Europeans conquered this land. Asiatics or Moors are descendants of Moroccans born in America. There is a myth that all Asiatic Moors were from Africa, which is not the truth. America is actually northwest Africa, and we are the native people of this land.

Europeans came over to America in 1492, annihilated the Indians—who were originally Moors—and changed our native language to English. They gave us Christianity, robbed us of our land and businesses, and changed the way we ate and the foods we ate. One of the foods they introduced was the pig. It goes by many names, including pig, swine, hog, and pork. The pig is one of the filthiest animals to consume. It has many parasites, and even after cooking it at high temperatures, the parasites are still in the flesh. During a parasite cleanse, you can see parasites or worms in the person's bowel movement! Herbal remedies and cleanses can show how you are eating the flesh of an animal—and whatever the animal eats.

As slaves, we were forced to make scraps out of pork and other animals to survive. It wasn't because we were supposed to eat that kind of food. Of course, being very creative with flavors, Asiatics prepared pork and other animal delicacies. A lot of Asiatics were not accustomed to that diet, and our bodies cannot handle that kind of food consumption.

There is a story in the Bible about Jesus casting the demons out of the pigs:

> And the swine, though he divide the hoof, and he clovenfooted, yet he cheweth not the cud; he is unclean to you. (Leviticus 11:7 KJV)

> And when he was come to the other side into the possessed with devils, coming out of tombs, exceeding fierce, so that no man might pass by that way. And behold they cried out, saying what have we to do with

thee, Je-sus thou son of God? art thou com hither to torment us before the time? And there was a good way off from them an herd of many swine feeding. So the devils besought him, saying, If thou cast us out, suffer us to go away into the herd of swine. And he said unto them, Go and when they were come out, they went into the herd of swine: and behold, the whole herd of swine ran violently down a steep place into the sea, and perished in the waters. (Matthew 8:28–33)

It's alarming how the source of our food has changed. Pigs, cows, and chickens are growing very quickly for human consumption and to keep the food chain growing. The animals are not being fed just corn and grass; they are being fed other types of feed and injected with steroids and hormones. That's why you can go into a grocery store and pick up a pack of chicken wings that are as big as your arm! Animals get sick with cancer and other diseases, but the grocery chains cut off the cancer or leave part of it on the flesh. When humans consume it, they can easily get cancer as the years go by.

The overconsumption of these acidic foods has created diseases that many Asiatics have come to believe run in the family. If a person's mother had heart disease or cancer, it will be passed down to the next generation. A person is not born with congestive heart failure or heart disease unless they have some kind of congenital heart disease that developed in the womb.

No one is born with chronic diseases! Unhealthy lifestyles can be adapted—or generational chains can be broken. Just because Grandma had diabetes doesn't mean that a family member in the fourth generation is going to get the disease. A person can break the generational sickness chain by adopting an alkaline-balanced lifestyle. No diet or lifestyle is 100 percent foolproof, but most illnesses can be prevented. Some illnesses are caused by external and environmental issues. There are harmful particles in the air, water, and earth. The way to keep balanced is by using vitamins, herbal remedies, spiritual meditation, and detoxing the body. This creates a fully alkaline-balanced lifestyle for the entire mind, body, and soul.

Our communities need to stop normalizing high blood pressure. We all endure stress in our daily lives, but blood pressure shouldn't be part of it. It's dangerous and deadly. It's not normal to have high blood pressure, especially when it comes to diet and lifestyle.

There is an old slave mentality that chronic diseases are hereditary. Food and any other external sources shouldn't damage the blood and the body's organs. Food should provide comfort and nutrition to the mind, body, and soul. They are all connected. If something causes more harm than good to your body, you should make a conscious effort to let go of whatever it is.

Making better health choices starts in the mental rolodex. Everything we eat or drink has energy. This energy can be positive or negative. It is produced in the body and spirit. It can create balance and calmness or obsessive cravings, restlessness, and irritability. We are whole beings, and we should eat foods that keep us that way. Nutrients and vitality keep us healthy.

An alkaline diet is the best nutritional route for a healthy body, especially a plant-based regime. The body is naturally able break down the plants and vitamins consumed and store them in the proper areas for health. Meat is not properly digested in the body, which causes mechanical and health issues. Human teeth are not able to chew the fibrous and toughness of the flesh being consumed.

Carnivores like lions and wolves have sharp teeth that can tear through flesh, and their bodies can naturally digest meat. Humans cannot, and our teeth are not sharp and have different shapes. Our bodies cannot naturally digest flesh. Some people have no health issues, but most people will develop them as time goes on. Not all plant-based foods are created equal. Some are processed—especially meat substitutes—and they have a lot of soy, preservatives, fillers, and sodium. It's best to be mindful and prepare fresh plant-based foods. Moderation is the key to any dietary lifestyle.

"Kidney kindness foods" are good for patients on dialysis. My personal favorites are tofu, apples, blackberries, grapes, and blueberries. Pears, plums, turnip greens, strawberries, cucumbers, jalapenos, seaweed, kelp, onions, garlic, mushrooms, pineapples, cherries, and cranberries are great for maintaining healthy blood pressure and low sodium levels.

CHAPTER 5

Knowing Your Diet

The power of a diet is very important for a various amount of reasons. The food for public consumption holds a gargantuan influence overall with maintaining the levels of your optimal health. There are foods that feed the body the nutrients that it needs for the activity of the brain and the connection to the body. The body cannot survive without the mind. Most of the public does not know what a balance diet consist of and is looked through the prism of losing weight. Weight gain or loss is not the only factors when it comes to evaluating a person's diet. It is important for the masses to properly be educated on this subject matter to raise the level of consciousness and eradicate all of the epidemics that has plagued humanity.

—Michael Simpson-El Jr.

There are many great recipes; some are old, and some are new. The food system has changed historically and culturally in the past three hundred years. Many of the true inhabitants' cultural food systems have been taken away through enslavement. They have been replaced with the adoption of another culture that is not connected to their forefathers and foremothers.

The USDA and FDA explains the foods that the population consumes. The foundation of nutrition has been stripped from the education curriculum. The board's administration has been adamantly opposed to adding hours to the health curriculum across the board, especially for doctors and surgeons. The resistance has had a significant effect on the proliferation of chronic disease and human deficiencies. The balance of food and medicine need to be restored.

> The relationship between food and medicine goes hand in hand. This is the era of time now every disease, sickness and deficiency are treated with some type of pill. Prior to the changes of the health care profession natural remedies was the care of the day. Most people that work in the medical field today are not even aware of natural remedies and are frowned upon on platforms concerning public health, therefore explaining what methods would cure certain ailments. There are some plants that provide instant remedies such as dandelion root which would cleanse the liver and other vital organs of the body. Now a pill would produce this same effect but the body would suffer from a side effect of that pill. This is a great concern because this pill fixed one problem and created another.

> The war on drugs changed to industries simultaneously regarding law enforcement and health care. The two events gave birth to the person industrial complex and the legalized drugs known as pharmaceutical companies "big pharma." One of the major government agencies the CIA denied its involvement on the war of drugs. The war on drugs was a time period where drugs were being smuggled into the United States for America through certain parts of the country. This created mass destruction in the streets among predominately Asiatic communities. These crimes and the lack there of feed the beast of the prisons. Supply and demand is

very simple the supply is the prison system the demand is the so called drug peddlers. The CIA had direct involvement in the process by their own admission after a book that was published called *Dark Alliance* by Gary Webb. This book uncovered the CIA involvement, the contras, and crack cocaine explosion. Barry Seal was a pilot that contracted drug trafficking through the port of Arkansas with the governor at the time Bill Clinton. This phenomenon changed the way people were medicated and the food industry. The question is why is this information relative to the diet of millions of Americans. These events change the whole dynamic of the health care system. The war on drugs legitimately expanded the pharmaceutical giant and the medication to the public that looks for remedy when they become ill. This is a major atrocity and we have no one to blame but these selected officials. The people have to make the change for a more healthy society and take back the power. The constitution demands this action because it states first "We The People!" (Michael Simpson-El Jr.)

Kidney failure and hypertension affect all age groups, but they are running rampant for people in their twenties, thirties, forties and fifties. Most health organizations are telling people to watch their blood pressure numbers, but they aren't leaning toward more natural options for blood pressure issues. Why is this? They will tell you to take a pill every day for hypertension, but it all starts with the high fat content and other toxins in the blood that are creating the high pressure and imbalance in the blood.

More Asiatics are starting to wake up to better health. They are going back to growing gardens, taking natural remedies, eating more alkaline foods, and taking nutritional supplements. This is definitely a positive sign that people are saying no to bad foods that create illness and disturbances in our bodies. They are becoming more spiritual and more aligned with the universe and feeling whole within themselves. This is an empowering feeling to have, and it creates more healthy options for the generations after us. We are not passing down generational curses, we are passing down generational health and wealth.

Natural remedies do not create side effects; they produce results as long as they aren't mixed together. A holistic doctor or practitioner can assist with those needs to naturally eradicate health issues. Side effect could vary, depending on the type of medication. Health care is treating the symptoms and not the cure! With the influence of pharmaceutical companies, it is very difficult to find a person who practices the ways of the ancient ones. Curing the body from any sickness or disease is not a goal of the practitioners of medicine. The greatest wealth on the planet is your health.

There are seven major organs in the body, and the food that is consumed determines how those organs will function. Fruits and vegetables are supposed to be the basis of an adequate diet. Plant-based diets are very high in vitamins, minerals, and botanicals. These diets are directly related to health and what food is being consumed daily.

Digestion starts in the mouth; therefore, the focus is concentrated on chewing. The mandible is the mechanism that processes the food into the body. The human body is not designed to eat flesh because the teeth are not equipped to properly chew the flesh so that it can be digested properly.

When having a conversation, things must be called by their correct names. We must call things by what they actually are. When you ask people about absorbing vitamin D, most would say that you receive Vitamin D from dairy products. You receive Vitamin D from the sun and various fruits and vegetables. When talking about meat, it is important that we distinguish the meat of an animal from the meat of an apple, peach, pear, or plum. Flesh is not meat because it is produced by the slaughter of an animal or human.

Hospital Administrations have a strong foundation with the medication as means of treatment and control. This is all backed by World Health Organization and the CDC because these organizations are the ones leading the charge. This is why the health profession is constructed a certain way and how drugs are pushed at an alarming rate. Most patients that are based in the setting of a hospital are presented with some form of medication. Now this practice presents an option but not a remedy. Most medications involve heroin, oxycodone or both. The foundation of most drugs stems from opioids which coincides with the war on drugs. The drugs where being smuggled through certain ports of the United States for America. The impact that these drugs has had on the people of this continent is repulsive and is a major atrocity. This practice has produced addictions to these medications are a driving force for crime, medical malpractice and overdosed. (Michael Simpson-El Jr.)

Dr. Sebi wrote *How to Naturally Detox the Liver, Reverse Diabetes and High Blood pressure through Dr. Sebi Alkaline Diet."* Dr. Sebi was a Honduran man with a very humble beginning. He was known as an herbalist, a pathologist, and a naturalist in different regions of the world. Dr. Sebi invented and established effective treatments for diabetes and hypertension, and organ cleansing is still helping millions of people with these conditions of the world.

Dr. Sebi said there were six fundamental food groups: live, raw, dead, hybrid, genetically modified, and drugs, but his diet basically cut out all the food groups except live and raw food, thereby encouraging dieters to eat as closely to a raw vegan diet as possible. These foods include naturally grown fruits and vegetables and whole grains. He believed that raw and live foods were electric, which fought the acidic food waste in the body. So, with his approach to eating, Dr. Sebi established a list of foods that he decided were best for his diet. Dr. Sebi high blood pressure. He said, "Every high blood pressure drug in the market imitates water."

Dr. Sebi shared helpful tips to avoid high blood pressure:

- Avoid overeating even the healthiest food.
- Avoid salty foods as much as possible because they transform into plaque in the artery walls.

- In essence, avoid sodas, baking soda, soy sauce, and meat tenderizers.
- Never eat canned foods.
- Eliminate dairy products, sodium, cheese, and alcohol from your diet.
- Do not eat in the evening.
- Avoid every other type of rice except wild rice and brown rice.
- Alkaline grains are amaranth, fonio, kamut, quinoa, rye, and spelt.

Vitamins A, C, E, K, minerals, and a plant-based diet add health to the as hair, skin, and nails. Herbs that contain natural alkaline and that are high in minerals help open blood vessels and artery walls, and they eliminate plaque from the artery walls as well.

Detoxes include black seed oil, lemon, water, moringa, soursop, burdock, dandelion, aloe vera, honey, sea moss, which has more than ninety-two vitamins and minerals for the body fennel, oregano, basil, yellow dock, and cayenne—and many others. Healthy seasonings— achiote, basil, bay leaf, cayenne, cloves, dill, habanero, onion powder, oregano, powdered seaweed, pure sea salt, sage, savory sweet basil, and tarragon—keep blood pressure balanced and within a normal range. These vitamins and herbs should be taken on a daily basis for optimal health. A lifestyle that heals the body will reduce mucus-forming agents that cause sickness in the body.

People have experienced severe colds and flu like illnesses with chest and respiratory issues. Just like with any virus, you have to destroy it with heat and anti-inflammatory products. Hot herbal teas and the right electric, alkaline hot foods with herbs and spices, and vitamins and herbs with plenty of alkaline water flush the body of impurities, harmful bacteria, and toxins!

Immunity starts in the digestive system with the various probiotic and good and bad bacteria that keep gut flora functioning. To keep the body healthy and to keep the good bacteria healthy and flush out the bad, a person has to maintain balance to keep the immune system from breaking down and viruses and diseases from entering and suppressing the immune system.

Disease and mucus start in the colon and eventually move into the respiratory and other membranes. The environment inside the body is acidic, which helps viruses and bacteria breed and grow. The unnatural mucus agents like heavy accumulation of dairy products, animal flesh, environment factors, and cigarettes attack the body's defenses, causing the immune system to be low and defenseless. The viruses multiply and take on different formations.

Vitamins and natural, raw foods are essential for cleaning your blood, and we should detox often to keep the body's systems healthy. Cleaning your blood definitely helps with uncontrolled high blood pressure, which erodes the arteries and other blood and nutrient vessels that provide oxygen to the body. Eradicate toxins and flush toxins out of the body on a daily basis. I'm not saying that one cannot get viruses, but if they do, it will be very brief and not severe, especially with the herbal remedies listed above for non-renal individuals.

Renal (kidney) patients have to be cautious when consuming herbs and certain foods. Some foods contain high amounts of potassium and phosphorus and can become detrimental to their hearts and bones. These herbs must be used in moderation and not mixed with medications. There is light at the end of the tunnel if people believe and do the right thing for their bodies.

Growing up in the nineties, I was very slim. I ate all types of unhealthy junk food, but my mother's home-cooked meals were always healthy with meat, carbs, and vegetables. Sometimes they weren't, and there was a balance. My favorites were twenty-five-cent beef slim jims, fried skins, hot potato chips, chocolate candies, and pop. My cousins, friends, and I used to play outside a lot, especially during the summer months. We used to burn off a lot of that unhealthy junk food. As a child, I was not gaining weight. I was carefree, and I wasn't aware of what those foods were doing to me. All I knew was they tasted good, and it was all fun and living life.

In my twenties, I began to have high cholesterol and high blood pressure issues. My favorite foods were hard salami, fried mozzarella sticks, fried bacon, pepperoni, fried chicken, and roast. I ate these foods frequently, and they made me gain weight and have dizziness. I still enjoyed these foods despite how they made me feel. I didn't know any better and felt like I didn't have to do better with my diet. In my family, every health problem was blamed on genetics—and there was nothing anyone could do about it. We are taught that chronic diseases were passed down from generation to generation. They said it was "in your blood." That statement is very powerful. We can control what's in our blood and how we clean it and keep it healthy to live our best lives.

I had to rid my body of beef and pork because they made my blood pressure go up. I felt dizzy, and they were hard to digest, which caused constipation. It was not good for my body, and I feel a difference with not consuming those foods. When I was pregnant with my first son, I was diagnosed with pregnancy hypertension. I ate all types of fried foods, and my favorites were deep-fried pork chops and pizza. I was eating whatever I wanted because I was pregnant with cravings. What baby wants, baby gets! I really didn't take my blood pressure seriously because I was expecting a child. It caused me to have significant swelling and weight gain. It almost caused me to have preeclampsia, a medical condition where high blood pressure affects the mother and fetus, causing stroke, seizures, early delivery, or even death.

After I gave birth to a healthy, beautiful boy, I knew I needed to take control of my blood pressure and health. The first step was to stop eating fleshy, fried foods.

In 2017, my husband proclaimed his nationality and birthright. I followed suit in 2018. It was a legal and lawful process that recognized and identified us as Moorish American. We are the original people to this land. America is also known as Amexem and Egypt of the West. We were naturalized under the direction and guidance of the Moorish School of Law and History under the excellent leadership and direction of National Grand Sheik, The Moorish Science Temple, The Divine and National Movement of North America, Inc. #13, and The Moorish American National Republic (www.Moorish American National Republic.com).

The El in my last name is my ancient Hebrew title. My husband and sons also proudly have it. This is one of the most uplifting and rewarding decisions Michael and I have ever made. We learn about who we are as a people and culture as well as learning about uplifting fallen humanity. We go to a health food store every week. They sell all-natural, organic herbs, supplements, and plant-based foods We were so intrigued with their products that I began taking natural remedies to lower my blood pressure and cholesterol levels. I take a natural bitters liquid formula. Essential Palace Organic Black Seed Living Bitters is a miraculous detox herbal bitter that lowers cholesterol and blood pressure. I take a teaspoon a day thirty minutes before I eat breakfast or drink alkaline coffee, which helps me.

I was impressed and didn't have to take dangerous blood pressure medicine. That was a relief. I felt more in control of my health because there are many natural ways to control hypertension. I also began to eat more vegetarian and vegan dishes, which helped with my blood pressure and digestion. My body started to feel more energized and better, and even my skin was clearer. I also started cooking more vegetarian dishes at home. My family loved it, and the meat substitutes like tofu and mushrooms made pepper steak dishes taste amazing!

I maintained the same diet when I was pregnant with my second son. My blood pressure was better since I slowed down with eating fried foods. I barely ate any animal flesh. When I was pregnant with my third son, I ate more vegetarian grains, breads, rice, and fish. I was asked if my baby was receiving enough protein. People said, "That baby needs meat to survive! You can't survive without meat!" I took vitamins and ate plant protein, and my baby was healthy and strong!

My blood pressure was a lot better, and I received a lot of exercise since I still was working until thirty-eight weeks. Malik was very healthy, and he grew fine in my womb. He made his grand entrance into the world with no medicine, no epidural, and no birthing coach in his daddy's arms! My loving husband, "Dr. Daddy", delivered our son Malik in the car! A woman can carry a child and eat a plant-based diet. It can be done. Plant-based foods have more vitamins, calcium, iron, and nutrients than the average steak or glass of milk. You are your healthiest and best self without all the unnecessary health issues.

I have continued to live my best life with this dietary lifestyle, and it is one of the best decisions I have made in my entire life. I feel better. I've lost weight. I've gained a lot of clarity about what to put in my body, and that created a natural openness to my spirituality about life and nutrition. I'm far from perfect, and I still have a lot of work to do in terms of my health, but I'm on the right path. I'm taking it one day at a time, and my improvements will flourish over time.

How do I receive protein and nutrients if I don't eat meat or limit my consumption of animal protein? I eat more vegetarian food and some vegan food. I consume chicken and fish now and then, but even that animal flesh is limited. I'm personally working on eliminating meat out of my dietary lifestyle.

Society has brainwashed us so much that if you say you don't consume a particular food, a person is given a side-eye or a perplexed look. People are so consumed with tradition that they aren't even aware of where these traditions originated, their true meaning, and how they play out in their lives. When something is presented to us that's been around for more than a hundred years, we should just go with the flow and pass those ideologies down to the next generations. Asiatics didn't start having blood pressure issues until we started consuming the salty and sugary foods that we were introduced to. It's no wonder why people say high blood pressure runs in families because we continue to pass those traditions and food to future generations. They have to be broken.

Slowly but surely, they are being broken. People are getting wiser about their health. Vegetarian and vegan foods and dishes are available in grocery chains and restaurants. People are starting to eat less meat and are seeing results in their strength, the way they feel, and their body composition. People say that not consuming animal flesh makes them feel lighter in the way they walk. They have more energy, and they have a lower appetite. Meat does not taste the same to them because they don't consume it often or haven't eaten it in a long time. They are eating all kinds of meat alternatives, including wheat gluten, pea protein, and plant protein. Mushrooms are a wonderful meat alternative. They have a chewy, fulfilling taste and texture and lots of flavor when prepared with herbs and spices.

People are also more aware that a better dietary lifestyle lowers their blood pressure and cholesterol. People are not eating like they used to. They want better for their bodies, and they want their children to be healthy. Children learn how to eat well from their parents. They don't have to consume cow's milk for calcium when almond milk has twice the calcium without all the hormones and steroids, making our kids develop faster and creating mucus and respiratory issues in their young bodies.

There are all types of children-friendly snacks. Plant-based chicken nuggets taste like real meat chicken nuggets, and they plenty of protein. They are processed and shouldn't be eaten all the time because of the preservatives, but they are a healthy alternative when you want to give your child a quick snack. Nothing is perfect, and eating too much of anything is not always a good thing. A good start can go a long way, and moderation with any food is key!

Dialysis treatment centers are appearing on almost every corner in the inner cities, like churches and liquor stores. More than 90 percent of dialysis patients are Asiatics, and the average patient is between twenty and fifty. A high number of older Asiatics—both men and women—are on dialysis. Kidney failure affects young and old people. A lot of them are on dialysis because of years of diabetes, heart disease, and other chronic illnesses that damaged or impaired their kidneys. Blood pressure is still a big factor because it affects the circulation and blood flow to the kidneys and the rest of the body. Some patients are on dialysis because of an imbalance in the body that caused "sleeping kidneys." They need to wake up with some type of herbal or medical intervention.

Kidney failure is becoming more and more rampant in our communities. It's almost as if it is a new normal. Some people think there's "something in the water." In the dialysis units, family members young and old are on dialysis. Patients become friends, and some date or have relationships because the patients have to go to treatment three times a week. Technicians and nurses see them often and develop professional patient interactions. You may consider them family, and they will treat you the same way.

Dialysis has its own little world, a world of all kinds of complex medical issues compacted to one individual spinning around in a machine. Patients are prescribed blood pressure medicines and medicines to help with phosphorus and calcium levels to keep their other organs healthy and stable during dialysis. Patients come to treatment with bags of pills and medications—along with issues from home or nursing facilities. Dialysis has so many different layers of treatment and care for patients.

African Americans develop chronic kidney disease and pulmonary hypertension (PH) at disproportionately high rates. Little is known whether PH heightens the risk of heart failure (HF) admission or mortality among chronic kidney patients including patients with non-end-stage renal disease.

> African Americans suffer the widest gaps in chronic kidney disease outcomes compared to Caucasian Americans and this is because of the disparities that exist in both health and healthcare. In fact the prevalence of CKD is 3.5 times higher in African Americans compared to Caucasian Americans. The disparities exist at all stages of CKD Importantly AAs are 10 times more likely to develop hypertension related kidney failure and 3 times more likely to progress to kidney failure.[1]

In May 2017, I started my new career as a hemodialysis technician with Greenfield Health Systems. I was very nervous, and just like any new person, I wanted to find my rhythm and learn the roles of the job quickly. I wanted to be the best hemodialysis technician I could be. The unit I started in was one of the biggest units in the state of Michigan. We see up to three hundred patients per week.

This job definitely takes a toll on one's mental, physical, emotional, and spiritual health. This fast-paced job requires cleaning chairs and dialysis machines between patients, cleaning blood of toxins, calculating patients' dry weight and fluid removal, using aseptic techniques, cannulating, properly placing needles in patients' fistulas or arm grafts. We must connect their needles to the blood lines that are attached to the machines

---

[1] "Pulmonary Hypertension is Associated with a Higher Risk of Heart Failure Hospitalization and Mortality in Patients with Chronic Kidney Disease: The Jackson Heart Study." *American Journal of Nephrology,* Selvaraj S; Shah SJ; Ommerborn MJ, Clark CR; Hall ME; Mentz RJ; Qazi S; Robbins JM; Skelton TN; ChenJ; Gaziano JM; Djousse L. Circulation; Heart Failure. 10 (6), 2017 Jun. UI 286111272017 S. Karger AG, Basel.

and make sure the machines are programmed to the proper settings. We try to make them as comfortable as possible. Seeing the patients' blood and lives going through the machines gives me chills sometimes. It makes me feel so grateful to be able to give them the best treatment possible.

As technicians and nurses, we see these patients come and go, and it's important that we take care of our own mental and physical health so that we don't become victims. Kidney disease can happen to anyone, and it's not always a dietary issue. It's crucial that we be good role models to these patients, especially when we take care of them and give them advice about their health. We have to learn to take our own advice.

It's very easy to become so consumed with work that we take our own health for granted, thinking that kidney failure cannot happen to us. When my shift is over, I leave the stress and demands of work and not bring those issues home to my family. A hot shower, good wholesome food, laughter, spending time with my family, and a good night's rest usually help me de-stress after a long day's work.

A hot shower, good wholesome food, laughter, spending time with my family, and a good night's rest usually help me de-stress after a long day's work. I'm always praying for my patient's healing and personal situations. At the end of my work shift I go home with ease and comfort knowing that I took diligent care of my patients. I prepare for the next day with a fresh start to continue care.

Meditation and prayer are great ways to let go of negative and unnecessary stress. I keep all my patients in my prayers because they need positivity and kindness while going through dialysis. They encounter other personal issues at home and in life in general.

After four years as a dialysis technician, I wanted to become the change and light to these patients. I have come to love and assist complete strangers with their dialysis care. I had to overcome many obstacles. I was told that I wouldn't make it that far at the unit and that I wouldn't become a technician who patients would want to cannulate and give them their treatment. Being a new technician at the time there were negative and unnecessary comments made by some of my peers. Some thought that I wouldn't make it being a good technician on the floor. Others were encouraging and said that I will do well. I persevered and believed in myself more with confidence. I pushed through the adversary and maintained being the best technician I possibly could. I stayed the test of time and continue to work hard, and I was able to reach goals and break through barriers that I didn't think I could maintain. I am able to use my personal experiences with my mother as my first renal patient to give my patients the best care possible.

CHAPTER 6

Kidney Health, Wellness and Healing

The dialysis unit is like a second home to a lot of patients, especially the ones who have been there for a number of years. Dialysis techs and nurses become like family since we see patients three times a week and maybe a fourth day if they have to have an extra treatment to remove extra fluids. Some patients consider the dialysis staff family because they see us more than their biological families. Most patients want to see a familiar, smiling face at their dialysis treatment and go home or back to the nursing facility.

A lot of patients who are new to dialysis are in denial, and they are struggling mentally with what has happened to them. These patients become depressed during this abnormal time in their lives. There are patients who are in so much denial that they skip dialysis treatments and continue living their lives like nothing is wrong with them—not realizing that their lives depend on this machine. Dialysis social workers can assist patients with the psychological effects of dialysis and even transportation to get to and from their treatments.

Since my beloved mother was one of these dialysis patients, the kindness and treatment that I give them are at a heart-to-heart level. I like to take my time with asking them how they are feeling and not just how they are doing. Asking them how they feel is a more realistic and caring question to ask them.

I give the utmost respect to them because these patients are a clear reminder that my mother was one of these patients at one point if time. Most patients appreciate that, and if they tell you that they feel a certain way, such as sad or tired, I usually can give them a good answer. I like my patients to know that I truly care about their well-being and that I'm not just there to receive a paycheck. Patients truly appreciate that extra level of care and concern. It gives them hope and something to look forward to: better health and a possible kidney transplant.

Sitting on a machine is not easy. Your whole life is being circulated, and blood is being cleaned of toxins. It's a risk that can also be taken away, depending on how the body responds to the treatment. The blood clotting in the machine, especially more than once, sets a patient up for receiving blood transfusions, severe anemia, fatigue, and eventually death. Patients become very scared and unstable. When the alarms go off, most patients panic and ask what is wrong. I really can't blame them because their lives depend on their treatment and care.

Patients are also depressed because they are missing time with their families, especially the ones who have children and grandchildren For patients who don't have families, going to dialysis is like having a family because they connect with the dialysis techs and nurses. Male patients can experience depression because of a lack of libido or not being able to maintain an erection, which can definitely put a strain on a relationship or a marriage. The female patients of childbearing ages, especially the ones in their twenties and thirties, who want to have children cannot because dialysis is very straining on a mother and unborn child. Most likely, the unborn child and mother would have to be dialyzed every day!

It is important that patients maintain a good rapport with the unit social worker.

> Your social worker is an essential part of your care.
> Their goal is to address your well-being and adjustment
> to dialysis. They provide support in all areas of your life,
> including, emotional, financial, and lifestyle.

Providing supportive counseling by helping you enhance your coping skills.

Providing education about kidney disease and referrals to resources.

Assisting with keeping or obtaining insurance coverage and transportation.

Evaluating for vocational rehabilitation services, including employment, going to school, volunteering, or returning to previously enjoyed activities.

Assisting you with understanding your patient rights and responsibilities and advanced care planning.

Helping you set goals and look to your future. (Greenfield Health Systems: Knowing Your Social Worker)

They are depressed because they don't have as much energy as they had prior to dialysis. A lot of their physical features have changed, including weight loss, darkening of the skin, hair loss, and fatigue. Some patients find different coping mechanisms for their new abnormal, and the depression that patients experience might be masked under a smile or a pleasant conversation. The technician or nurse may never know what these patients endure at home or before and after their dialysis treatments.

On top of being a dialysis technician, I listen and support patients. A kind word and a smile can go a long way. These patients go through more trials and tribulations than we could ever know. They like to discuss their lives before entering the world of dialysis and what they are going through. Some patients ask about my personal life and my family, but I always keep it professional and maintain a level of privacy.

Four years as a dialysis technician, I wanted to become the change and light to these patients I have come to love and assist. I had to overcome many obstacles, but I remain strong and determined because I know this profession is about someone else's care. I believe in myself more. I know what I can achieve. I created a more positive approach to my job duties, and I continued to do what I came here to do: take care of my patients safely and respectfully.

I've had a lot of mixed experiences as a dialysis technician. Some positive and some negative, but a positive attitude and learning and studying dialysis will get you far. This is definitely not an easy job; it is stressful, complex, and dangerous. Another person's life is your hands. Main veins and arteries in their heart or their arms are in your hands for care.

This is a life-or-death situation. The level of care and precision in treatment can determine a patient's fate before, during, and after treatment. Any mistake can damage their access site, recirculate the blood, or remove too little or too much fluid. We monitor low and high blood pressures and monitor patients' condition and mental states. We check if they are oriented, stable, confused, or have dementia.

If you been working at the unit for some time, knowing your patients can really help in their treatment. Even if the patient is new to the unit, learning about how much fluid they can remove, dry weight, being an AKI patient, and about the kind of treatment they need is vital as well. My experiences build good rapport with patients through trusting them with their care, positive conversations, laughter, and sometimes sentimental moments in their lives. They like to share with their "go-to technician" for needle placement and treatment.

Dialysis is very unpredictable; it can be a good thing or a bad thing. Some patients are doing well with their treatments, coming in for every session, and following their diet and fluid regimes, but something tragic happens to them. Dialysis isn't always to blame for a patient's death. Underlying conditions and freak accidents take their lives, which makes the grieving process very hard. Patients and staff members can develop close bonds. Some patients go to the hospital or pass away at home. Dialysis is like one big family, and it's like losing a loved one, which can affect everyone's mental health. When patients pass away, it. can be hard for other patients and staff members to function. We may know what comes with the nature of the job, but nothing can prepare anyone for life's tragedies.

A woman in her thirties walked into the dialysis unit, and I asked if she was there to pick up her grandmother.

She said, "No, I'm here from the vascular floor. This is my first day of dialysis treatment."

I was shocked, but I stayed calm. I smiled, took her to her dialysis chair, checked with the nurse about her information, checked her vitals, and made sure she was stable before I started the dialysis machine. The patient was quiet and looked worried. I gently cleaned her catheter and ran her blood through the machine. I continued to check her vitals and remove the minimum amount of fluid from her body.

I tried to make her as comfortable as possible by informing her about the process of dialysis and treatment she was receiving. I asked her how she ended up on dialysis.

She had been partying and drinking every weekend with her friends and eating whatever she liked. She was young and thought she could do whatever she wanted—and nothing would happen to her. She woke up one morning with severe back pain. She couldn't get out of bed, and she felt very sick. When she arrived at the hospital, the doctors ordered blood work and a urinalysis. Her blood pressure was very high, like 200/120, and she couldn't believe she was at stage one kidney failure. She thought only old people had that disease and wondered how it could happen to her. She was definitely in denial about her condition.

I told her it was common for Asiatics and their dietary lifestyle.

She didn't want to do dialysis and wondered how she could get off of it.

I told her she could change her diet to an alkaline diet, drastically reduce salty and sugary foods, watch her fluids, work out, and get adequate rest. If her kidneys got worse, she would have to wait for a kidney transplant.

The patient got her blood pressure under control and received a kidney transplant a few years later.

Another patient was kind of bizarre. He was listed as a patient with an acute kidney injury (AKI). Both of his kidneys failed and were temporarily asleep because he fell on some ice. The patient was on dialysis for a few weeks, and his kidneys eventually healed themselves. The patient was off of dialysis and was able to return to his normal life.

The body can heal itself, and some kidneys restart on their own after being diagnosed with acute kidney injuries. Kidneys can be wrapped in a cocoon of mucus, and an unhealthy balance disrupts their natural function. The kidneys can restart themselves, and some patients have experienced normal kidney function without ever needing kidney transplant. A patient with normal kidney function after dialysis will need to keep an alkaline-balanced, healthy blood pressure all the time.

Stress and meditation can lower blood pressure and maintain peace and comfort in proper oxygenated levels. Mental health is everything. It is your very existence. In the eighties and nineties, commercials referred to a mind on drugs being a terrible waste. Well, your mind is a terrible thing to waste with overconsumption of salt, sugar, and fried and acidic foods. These all affect blood pressure. Alkalinity in your diet keeps you aligned with the universe. Being calm and positive can help you make the right decisions about your health.

Positive energy helps oxygenated blood flow and keeps the body systems calm. That lets them do their functions properly. Carbon dioxide is released. Mind, body, and soul are one with the correct energy, and blood pressure affects all the natural energies the body produces. Negative energy creates stress in the body and can cause imbalances in the body, creating opportunities for low immune function and diseases to make a home there.

Exercise is one of the main keys to maintaining healthy blood pressure because it regulates and keeps the heart strong and pumping blood throughout the body. Exercise helps burn fat and sugar and releases toxins through the skin. Exercise gets the blood pumping. It sends nutrient-rich blood to the organs, and normal maintenance of blood pressure keeps it in the normal range.

Sleep is very important for healthy blood pressure. The body needs time to relax and rejuvenate cells and blood flow within itself. Blood pressure can remain high and unstable without rest. The heart needs to be able to pump blood effectively through its chambers and circulate through the rest of the body. The body stays young and rejuvenated. It's important for mental and emotional health. When you get enough sleep, you are able to be relaxed with stable blood pressure and a sense of clarity and ease. This is good for meditation and a calm sense of well-being. The mind, body, and spirit are able to manifest in the universe.

Water is the element that is just as important as blood. Water keeps the blood and nutrients flowing through the bloodstream, and it helps regulate temperature and homeostasis within the body. Water is so important for the body. It's vital for the kidneys because it helps flush them and regulates the urine pH. Water keeps the kidneys healthy and allows the toxins and urea to be flushed through the urethra and released through the urine.

Without enough water being consumed on a daily basis, the kidneys will suffer. Patients may develop high blood pressure, dehydration of the skin, hair, and nails, backaches, muscle spasms, headaches, and fatigue. Our bodies are made up of 98 percent of water, and they need water to survive.

In the new age of technology and the age of knowing and seeking truth and knowledge, people are starting to wake up to what is real and what is fake. People are starting to become more conscious of what foods and supplements they are putting in their bodies. People are more physically active and are becoming more spiritually aware of their mental and belief systems in the world we live in. Those traditional belief systems and old eating habits are slowly but steadily starting to disintegrate.

The older generation still believes in those ways of eating and are stuck in their old belief systems. A lot of elders feel like they have lived their lives, and they think getting sick in old age is just the name of the game. They think things are meant to happen and they want to let God have his way if it's their time to go meet him.

Some people say, "When you know better, you will do better." That is wrong! Just because a person knows better doesn't mean they will do better and get it together. Knowing is half the battle, but the action is the real work. Subconsciously people will continue to do or eat whatever they love because it feels good or tastes good, but deep down, that subconscious feeling isn't accurate.

Other people say, "When you know better, you will do better or have it all together." Wrong again—no one has it all together. We make changes when something goes wrong within our bodies. People like to live carefree lives, and most people choose to make the right changes. Unfortunately, that change sometimes comes too late. The right decisions give a person a clearer vision.

When I tell patients how I changed my lifestyle and blood pressure issues by not consuming red meat or pork, some of them wonder what I eat on a regular basis, especially with meatless meals. When I tell people that my dietary lifestyle has changed, they ask how my children get protein? Instead of being upset with people and their comments, I give them clear and precise answers because people are unaware of what protein is. They don't know there is such a thing as plant protein, and it has much more nutrition than meat or animal flesh. My children receive protein and calcium from almond milk and beans and vegetables. Most of the patients don't believe that because they are so used to the diet and foods that they have been eating all of their lives. They don't believe that the foods they have consumed have taken a toll on their organs and overall lifestyle.

This is the conditioning that Asiatics continue to keep indoctrinated in their minds. The real change starts when a person decides to change. No one can put it in you or make you do anything. Blood pressure doesn't have to control one's life; it can be managed. Daily life affects blood pressure. Everything is regulated by blood pressure in a positive or negative way, and it's important to manage it correctly and effectively.

My own experiences with blood pressure issues have opened my eyes to better health on my physical and spiritual journey. I have learned what works for me and shared insights about what can work for others. Being a dialysis technician has made me more aware about optimal health. I am so much more aware of the importance of good blood pressure and how it affects overall well-being. When you know better, you will do better—at least that applies to most situations when the action is actually applied!

I'm very grateful to Father God Allah for the experience and opportunity to help others and do the missionary work to help heal my community. There is still a lot of work to be done to raise awareness about the deadly effects of hypertension, which leads to kidney failure and dialysis. It's a real thing, and it's not some kind of stigma. I just want to keep leading by example with better health.

Follow these healthy lifestyle tips to take charge of your kidney health:

1. Meet regularly with your health care team. Staying connected with your doctor, whether in person or using telehealth via phone or computer, can help you maintain your kidney health.

2. Manage blood pressure and monitor blood glucose levels. Work with your health care team to develop a plan to meet your blood pressure goals and check your blood glucose level regularly if you have diabetes.

3. Take medicine as prescribed and avoid NSAIDs like ibuprofen and naproxen. Your pharmacist and doctor need to know about all the medicines you take.

4. Aim for a healthy weight. Create a healthy meal plan and consider working with your doctor to develop a weight-loss plan that works for you.

5. Reduce stress and make physical activity part of your routine. Consider healthy stress-reducing activities and get at least thirty minutes of physical activity each day.

6. Make time for sleep. Aim for seven to eight hours of sleep per night.

7. Quit smoking. If you smoke, take steps to quit. (www.niddk. nih.gov health information/healthstatisitcs/kidneydisease)

Hypertension is reversible and treatable. We do not have to suffer in the dark. I am still a work in progress. With everything I have experienced, I've learned that everyone isn't going to agree with me. There is so much knowledge and information and healthy ways to protect our kidneys and bodies. This book was created to share my experiences and explain how hypertension is one of the biggest reasons why Asiatics suffer from so much kidney failure and dialysis. We need to do better as a community and a nation. The ratios for Asiatics and other races are significantly disproportionate. I'm a living witness to the harmful effects of hypertension. I want to be a leading example to assist with ways to protect your kidneys, love your kidneys, and heal your kidneys.

Kidney health and supportive material resources are available for people who are suffering from chronic kidney disease and end-stage renal failure. There are patient-to-patient support groups, peer mentor programs, kidney support groups, and workshops.

I want to continue to help others and become an advocate for change. Anyone can be diagnosed with kidney failure at any point of their lives. It starts with being more conscious of what we are consuming in our daily lives and dietary lifestyles and becoming more in control of our health. People need more farmers markets and proper nutritional education about how foods affect the kidneys and overall health.

After four years, I'm still working as a Certified Clinical Dialysis Technician at West Pavilion Outpatient Dialysis Unit. I never thought I would remain standing strong, and I am more proud of myself than ever. This career has been one of the most rewarding experiences I've ever endured. I don't have a single ounce of regret with the challenges I faced when I started my career. Along the way, I learned the pros and the cons of the job. One of the most rewarding opportunities is that I get a chance to help people receive their dialysis treatment safely and properly. I'm still learning and have so much learning and growing to accomplish. In the health care field, there is always room for progress. I have grown to love and care for people of all walks of life. I listen to their treatment goals and personal goals in life. I've learned that a smile, kindness, and encouragement can go a long way in helping patients get through any situation.

This life is so unpredictable, and it can take us on so many journeys and roads. It's a personal choice to travel a path of mental, physical, spiritual, and emotional wellness. I pray that I continue to be a beacon of light and love to others on the journey to fully complete your healing and wellness.

I believe that I was meant to become a dialysis technician to help others. I wrote this book in honor and memory of my beautiful mother, Cathy Ann Jones. Her dedication to health care and her unfortunate health struggles help me strive for greatness in my career. To all of my kidney dialysis patients at West Pavilion Dialysis in Detroit, I love and care for you all! It has been such an honor and a blessing to give so much of my heart and care to you. I didn't realize that it was my calling, and this profession has changed my life and outlook on life in so many ways.

A special gracious thank you to my husband, Michael Simpson-El, Jr., for his dedicated support, encouragement, love, and thoughtful input of words and knowledge in my book. I am truly thankful for an opportunity to help others in my community and in my family!

A special thank you to Greenfield Health System, Henry Ford Hospital, Supervisors and Nurse Manager at West Pavilion Outpatient Dialysis Unit, for the opportunity to provide patient care and assist patients in my community.

I pray that this book is an inspiration to my patients, my peers, my family, my friends, and everyone who is focusing on making positive changes and reinforcements in their daily lives for better health. You are becoming a whole person and showing your body and kidneys love and kindness. Peace and Love!

REFERENCES

The Naturalization Orientation Book: The Moorish Science Temple The Divine and National Movement of North America, Inc, No.13 The Moorish American National Republic.

The Holy Koran of the Moorish Science Temple of America Circle 7 Divinely prepared by the Noble Prophet Drew Ali.

Dr Sebi: Cure for Kidney Disease: A Comprehensive Guide on How to Cure Kidney Disease Using Dr. Sebi's Alkaline Eating Diet Method, Adam Lovren.

Greenfield Health Systems Dedicated to Dialysis Green Book.

Greenfield Health Systems Dedicated to Dialysis Pep Talk Patient Education Program pamphlet: "Fluids During the Summer."

Greenfield Health Systems:// http:// ghsrenal.com.

Dark Alliance, Gary Webb.

National Institute of Diabetes and Digestive and kidney Disease www. niddk.nih.govhealth information/healthstatistics/kidney disease.

Online Etymology Dictionary.

Black's Law Dictionary, fourth edition.

Greenfield Health Systems: Dedicated to Dialysis pamphlet: "Your Dialysis Social Worker."

The King James Holy Bible.

American Society of Nephrology.

www.nepro.com.

Pathophysiology for the Health Professions fourth edition, Barbara E. Gould and Ruthanna M. Dyer.

"Intradialytic hypertension: a less recognized cardiovascular complication of hemodialysis," *Am J kidney Dis.* 2010 Mar; 5S(3): 580- 9. Doi:10. 1053/j.ajkd.2009.08.013.epub 2009 Oct 22, Julia K Inrig.

"Epidemiology of Hypertension," *CKD Adv Chronic Kidney Dis.* 2015 Mar; 22 (2): 88–95.doi: 10.1053/j.ackd.2014.09.004, Bruce Horowitz, Dana Miskulin, Philip Zager.

Printed in the United States
by Baker & Taylor Publisher Services